Poison Dart Frogs as Pets

Poison Dart Frog Care, Behavior, Diet, Interaction, Costs and Health.

By

Ben Team

1

Table of Contents

Foreword

Famous for their kaleidoscopic colors and toxic skin secretions, poison dart frogs are some of the most interesting animals in the world. They've been revered by primitive hunter-gatherer cultures for centuries, and they've been featured in a variety of nature-oriented documentaries and films.

They always attract attention at zoos and nature centers who maintain living specimens, and nature lovers frequently spend hours starring at high-resolution photos of these gorgeous frogs.

It shouldn't be surprising then, that they've also become popular with pet keepers. And though they were only kept by a handful of experienced hobbyists in the past, poison dart frogs are nearly mainstream pets in amphibian keeping circles.

But keeping poison dart frogs requires plenty of preparation, and you'll need to learn quite a bit about these frogs before you add a few to your home. We'll try to help you do that in the following pages.

***

It bears mentioning that while some poison dart frogs living in the wild are quite dangerous to the touch, their captive-bred counterparts do not produce dangerous toxins. Most wild-caught poison dart frogs will stop producing dangerous secretions after a lengthy time in captivity too.

Although the exact mechanism by which poison dart frogs produce their toxins is not understood, most biologists who study these frogs suspect that the frogs are able to do so by sequestering alkaloids present in the bodies of their prey. These compounds are converted into toxins once in the frog's body.

Because the insects fed to captive poison dart frogs do not contain these alkaloids, the frogs are unable to produce their toxins. Accordingly, captive-bred poison dart frogs never produce toxins, and wild-caught individuals eventually run out of these alkaloids and cease producing their poisons for which they are famous.

Care is still wise when interacting with wild-caught individuals (as well as those of undetermined origin). For that matter, direct contact with most amphibians is generally best avoided. Many other amphibians produce toxic secretions (though they are rarely as dangerous as those produced by poison dart frogs), and the contact is almost always stressful for the animal.

***

Part of the appeal of poison dart frogs is the habitats they require. Most keepers maintain their poison dart frogs in natural-looking vivaria, complete with plants, forest-like soils, and water features.

These efforts aren't always necessary, but the difference between maintaining a utilitarian poison dart frog habitat and a complex vivarium is rather small. You'll put almost as much effort into a minimalistic enclosure as you would a rainforest-style vivaria, given the humidity requirements of these species.

It can be very rewarding (not to mention educational) to design and maintain well-planted vivaria. So, while we'll be focusing primarily on the frogs themselves in the following pages, we'll also talk about some of the basic principles of natural vivaria design too.

***

As you begin your adventure with poison dart frog just remember to continue learning as much as you can about them and their habitats. Scientists regularly make new observations and learn previously unknown aspects of their behavior and biology.

Some of these lessons may influence the ways in which keepers maintain their frogs. The husbandry of these animals is a perpetually evolving pursuit, and you should be willing to adapt your practices as new facts come to light.

About the Author

The author, Ben Team, is an environmental educator and author with over 16 years of professional reptile-keeping experience.

Ben currently maintains www.FootstepsInTheForest.com, where he shares information, narration and observations of the natural world.

PART I: POISON DART FROGS

Properly caring for any animal requires an understanding of the species and its place in the natural world. This includes digesting subjects as disparate as anatomy and ecology, diet and geography, and reproduction and physiology.

It is only by learning what your pet is, how it lives, what it does that you can achieve the primary goal of animal husbandry: Providing your pet with the highest quality of life possible.

Chapter 1: Poison Dart Frog Description and Anatomy

Although poison dart frogs exhibit quite a bit of diversity in terms of color pattern and size, most have fairly similar anatomy.

We'll discuss the major physical and anatomical characteristics of this group of amphibians below.

Size

Simply put, poison dart frogs are relatively small frogs. Some of the smallest dart frogs – such as the "thumbnail" dart frogs of the genus *Ranitomeya* – are approximately ½ inch (1.2 centimeters) long.

On the other hand, a few species, such as the golden poison dart frog (*Phyllobates terribilis*), reach about 2 inches (5 centimeters) in length.

Most species weigh only a few grams, although the largest species and specimens may approach 1 ounce (28 grams) in weight.

Color and Pattern

Poison dart frogs are widely celebrated for their bold and beautiful color patterns. Different species bear different colors and patterns, and there is even some variation among individuals belonging to the same species. In fact, some species are polymorphic, and produce young bearing several different color patterns.

Some species, such as the golden poison dart frog referenced above, are predominately clad in a single color (gold in this case). Others, such as the blue poison dart frog (*Dendrobates* tinctorius "*azureus*") and bumblebee poison dart frog (*Dendrobates leucomelas*) incorporate black markings over a single base color.

But many other poison dart frog species bear several different colors. For example, the "blue jeans" morph of the strawberry poison dart frog (*Oophaga pumilio*), features a red-colored torso, but their legs are covered in blue and black tones.

Some even have complicated color patterns, consisting of several different colors. For example, the dyeing dart frog (*Dendrobates tinctorius*) is covered in a complicated pattern of blue, indigo, yellow and black tones.

Body
Poison dart frogs have fairly typical anuran body plans. Most have relatively broad noses and moderately plumb bodies, but their legs – particularly their front legs -- are often rather long and thin.

Most poison dart frogs have relatively long digits, which often bear enlarged tips that help them to climb. Most species have four digits on their front feet and five digits on their rear feet. However, the fifth digit on the rear feet is often poorly developed.

Some poison dart frogs have a "boxy" body shape, in which the outlines of the pelvis are rather visible. Others appear rounder when viewed from the side.

Internal Organs
While the average dart frog keeper need not understand the internal anatomy of their pet enough to perform exploratory surgery, you should familiarize yourself with the basic internal anatomy of frogs.

In most respects, the internal anatomy of frogs is similar to that of other vertebrates, such as humans. Accordingly, special attention is warranted for those aspects that differ from those of most other animals.

Skeletal System

The skeletal system of most frogs basically resembles that of most other vertebrates, aside from a few important details.

As with most other vertebrates, frogs have both axial and appendicular skeletons. The skull, vertebral column and ribs form the axial skeleton, while the shoulder girdle, pelvic girdle and limbs comprise the appendicular skeleton.

However, the hips are elongated in many frogs and the pelvis features long bones, rather than the flattened pelvis bones many other vertebrates have. Additionally, the spinal column is shortened in frogs, and the neck is essentially absent.

Frogs also have greatly elongated foot bones. In some cases, the longest digits are comprised of bones which, when taken as a group, exceed the length of the leg bones.

Digestive System

The digestive system of dart frogs is similar to that of other amphibians, and, to a lesser extent, vertebrates in general.

Just inside the mouth likes the esophagus, which transports food to the stomach. From here, food passes through the small and then large intestines before being expelled from the vent.

The pancreas and spleen lie close to the stomach, while the gallbladder attaches to the liver, just as it does in most other vertebrates. However, the livers of frogs have widely separated lobes, which lie on each side of the body cavity.

Circulatory and Pulmonary System

In general, the circulatory and pulmonary systems of frogs are similar to those of other vertebrates.

Frogs inhale and exhale through their mouth or nose, while the trachea carries air to and from two lungs.

Like many other reptiles and amphibians, frogs have three-chambered hearts, which feature two atria and a single ventricle. One atrium accepts oxygenated blood from the lungs, while the other atrium receives oxygen-poor blood from the body.

Both atria pump blood into a single ventricle, which then pumps the blood into the rest of the body. Normally, as in many other animals with three-chambered hearts, this means that the frog's body receives a combination of oxygen-rich and oxygen-poor blood. However, ventricular folds help to prevent the two types of blood from mixing completely.

Urinary and Reproductive System

Frogs filter waste products from their bloodstream via their paired kidneys. They then store these waste products in the urinary bladder.

Poison dart frogs engage in external fertilization, so their reproductive systems are slightly different from those of most other vertebrates.

For example, most male frogs lack an intromittent organ. Instead, sperm are simply produced in a pair of testes, and transported to the cloaca via a structure termed the ureter.

A red-backed poison dart frog rests on a leaf.

Females have a pair of ovaries, in which eggs form. Once they're fully developed, the eggs travel to a pair of oviducts, in which they'll remain until it is time to mate.

A chamber called the cloaca serves as the exit point for all products of the urinary and reproductive systems. This includes urine from the bladder, waste from the large intestine, sperm from the testes and ova from the ovaries.

Most frogs mate by adopting a position called amplexus, in which the male climbs onto the female's back. The female then releases the unfertilized eggs (usually into a water source). At the same time, the male begins releasing sperm cells, which fertilize the newly released eggs from the female.

However, many poison dart frogs skip amplexus altogether. Instead, the male will start by discharging sperm into a small water source. After doing so, the female will deposit the eggs where they'll be fertilized.

Others exhibit a variation on the typical amplexus position. Instead of crawling on the female's back, the pair will adopt a vent-to-vent posture, while facing different directions.

Note that many poison dart frogs will engage in "wrestling matches" with members of their own sex. These types of interactions are often mistaken for amplexus by keepers.

Chapter 2: Poison Dart Frog Biology and Behavior

Poison dart frogs exhibit a number of biological and behavioral adaptations that allow them to survive in their natural habitats. And while the specific adaptations demonstrated vary from one species to the next, many are common to the group as a whole.

Growth Rate and Lifespan

The growth rate of poison dart frogs varies in relation to the amount of food they can acquire. Accordingly, because they benefit from essentially unlimited food, captive poison dart frogs usually grow much more quickly than their wild counterparts do.

Most poison dart frog eggs hatch in about 1 to 2 weeks. They'll then enter a tadpole stage, which takes 1 to 2 months to complete.

After completing the tadpole stage of their development, the tiny frogs leave the water and become terrestrial organisms. Different species exhibit varying sizes at the time of metamorphosis, but most are quite small and rarely longer than 1 inch (2.5 centimeters) in length.

The frogs will feed voraciously and grow over the subsequent months. It typically takes about 6 to 24 months for the young frogs to reach their adult size. From this point forward, the frogs will grow very little, if at all.

There isn't a great deal of data available regarding the typical lifespan of wild-living poison dart frogs. Most likely live about 3 to 5 years, but captive specimens often exceed these ages. Some have approached or exceeded 20 years of age, but such individuals are relatively rare. A typical captive lifespan for most poison dart frogs is likely in the neighborhood of 5 to 8 years.

Metabolism and Digestion

Frogs are ectotherms, who's metabolism varies with the ambient temperatures in which they live. The warmer the temperatures are, the faster the biological processes taking place inside the frog's body operate.

This essentially means that poison dart frogs will eat more and grow more quickly in warm habitats than they will in cold habitats.

However, in practice, the differences in metabolic rate and appetite are rather subtle. This is because poison dart frogs have evolved to live in tropical habitats, often under the dense canopy of a rainforest.

This effectively prevents them from having to cope with wildly varying temperatures – in most cases, the temperatures in the habitats of wild poison dart frogs fluctuate very little.

In fact, poison dart frogs can only survive in a fairly narrow temperature range, and many will become stressed (and potentialy die) if the temperatures rise above the mid-80s Fahrenheit (about 30 degrees Celsius).

Foraging Behavior

Poison dart frogs are relatively active feeders, who search for food in a small area of the rainforest floor. Unlike many other frogs, who prefer feeding on relatively few large prey items, poison dart frogs exhibit the opposite tendency. They generally survive by eating large numbers of very small prey items.

Most poison dart frogs in the wild probably eat every day or nearly so. However, well-fed adults can often go several days between meals in captivity.

Like most other frogs, poison dart frogs use a sticky tongue to catch prey. The tongue is connected to the front of their mouths, which helps provide greater range for this food-collecting tool.

Diel and Seasonal Activity

The majority of frog species are nocturnal animals, but poison dart frogs exhibit a diurnal activity pattern. This is likely related to their bold warning colors, which would not provide very much value if they moved about at night.

Most poison dart frogs live in regions that don't experience very pronounced seasonal changes with regard to temperature. However, many live in places where the humidity levels can change throughout the year.

Typically, poison dart frogs remain active all year long. However, they may become somewhat inactive during prolonged dry spells.

Defensive Strategies and Tactics

The primary way by which poison dart frogs protect themselves is through the combination of their poisonous skin secretions and bold coloration.

Unlike many other frogs, which tend to avoid moving out into the open (at least during the daytime), poison dart frogs often move brazenly through their habitats while searching for food or mates.

Most of the predators in the rainforest are susceptible to the skin secretions of the poison dart frogs, so the frogs needn't do much to avoid predation. However, there are a few predators that appear immune to their poisons. The frogs are typically rather helpless when trying to defend themselves from such predators, as they're incapable of fighting back in an effective way.

Reproduction

Like all other frogs, poison dart frogs begin life as eggs before hatching into a larval form, known as a tadpole. Tadpoles are typically aquatic, but thanks to the extremely damp nature of the rainforests in which they live, some poison dart frog tadpoles spend a portion of the time living in very shallow puddles or pools of water.

Many species spend their tadpole stage living inside pools of water that collect in flowers called bromeliads. They are often carried to these bromeliads by their mother, who will carry them on her back.

Poison dart frogs may breed at just about any time of year when the humidity is sufficiently high. Males typically begin calling from elevated perches, and they'll often fight with other males for the best perching locations.

Females typically have their choice of mates, and they usually pick males that have secured the best perches. However, some species also appear to value bright colors when picking mates.

Chapter 3: Classification and Taxonomy

Like all other living species, poison dart frogs are placed within a hierarchical classification scheme. The highest levels of this classification scheme help distinguish groups like vertebrates from others, while the lower levels of classification distinguish poison dart frogs from other frogs

As currently construed, poison dart frogs are classified as follows:

Kingdom: Animalia

Phylum: Chordata

Class: Amphibia

Order: Anura

Family: Dendrobatidae

All poison dart frogs are members of the family Dendrobatidae. However, the world's 170-odd species are grouped into several different genera, based upon their ancestry.

A few of the most important genera include:

- *Dendrobates*

- *Epipedobates*

- *Phyllobates*

- *Ranitomeya*

- *Oophaga*

Most of these genera contain multiple species. However, the exact number of species found in each genus fluctuates wildly.

For example, there are five species currently assigned to the genus *Dendrobates*, while *Hyloxalus* contains more than 50. On the other hand, at least one genus – *Minyobates* – contains only a single species.

A few of the most commonly kept poison dart frog species are listed below.

- Green and Black Poison Dart Frog (*Dendrobates auratus*)

- Bumblebee Poison Dart Frog (*Dendrobates leucomelas*)

- Dyeing Poison Dart Frog (*Dendrobates tinctorius*)

- Yellow-Striped Poison Dart Frog (*Dendrobates truncatus*)

- Phantasmal Poison Dart Frog (*Epipedobates tricolor*)

- Anthony's Poison Dart Frog (*Epipedobates anthonyi*)

- Golden Poison Dart Frog (*Phyllobates terribilis*)

- Black-Legged Poison Dart Frog (*Phyllobates bicolor*)

- Strawberry Poison Dart Frog (*Oophaga pumilio*)

Chapter 4: The Poison Dart Frog's World

Like all other species, poison dart frogs exist as part of a community of other organisms – they do not live in a vacuum. This not only includes other animals, including predators, prey and competitors, but plants, fungi and bacteria too.

We'll discuss some of these relationships below.

The Habitat and Range of Poison Dart Frogs

As with every other animal in the world, the habitat and range of poison dart frogs has influenced their history and biology significantly. We'll discuss their range and habitat below.

Range

All of the living poison dart frogs naturally hail from Central and South America. Their range includes parts of Panama, Costa Rica, Nicaragua, Suriname, Brazil, Columbia, Guyana, French Guyana, Peru, Venezuela, and Ecuador.

Poison dart frogs have also been introduced to several of the Hawaiian Islands. These feral animals are likely released pets and their descendants.

Habitat

The majority of poison dart frogs inhabit rainforests of one type or another. Some species live in the vast tracts of rainforest found in the Amazon Basin, while others inhabit small rainforest patches, which are surrounded by relatively dry savannah habitats.

Some poison dart frog species live in lowland habitats, which are essentially at sea level, while others are found ranging up into the cloud forests of highland regions.

Predators and Prey: The Poison Dart Frog's Food Web

The most notable interactions most animals have with other species are those which it eats, and those which try to eat them. We'll talk about both – predators and prey – of poison dart frogs below.

Prey

Poison dart frogs are carnivores, who primary feed on small arthropods. While the exact species poison dart frogs prey upon are not always known, the broad outlines of their diet are not in dispute.

A few of the most important food sources for poison dart frogs include:

- Crickets

- Roaches

- Springtails

- Ants

- Flies

- Beetles

- Insect larvae

- Spiders

- Mites

- Termites

- Slugs

Predators

Poison dart frogs have a few biological and behavioral adaptations that help them defend themselves from predators. However, it is their poisonous skin secretions which provide them with the most protection (along with their bold coloration, which serves to advertise their poisonous nature).

Nevertheless, there is at least one predator – the fire-bellied snake (*Erythrolamprus epinephelus*) -- is immune to their poisons and are therefore capable of consuming dart frogs.

It is possible that other predators have developed a tolerance or immunity to the poisons produced by dart frogs but have avoided the attention of biologists.

Bats, for example, are often important predators of many tropical frog species. However, this is unlikely in the case of poison dart frogs, as they're diurnal animals. It is possible that other snake species, as well as small predatory birds may consume poison dart frogs from time to time.

It is also important to note that different poison dart frog species produce different toxins, and just because the fire-bellied snake is capable of eating some poison dart frogs, does not mean that they can safely consume all species.

PART II: POISON DART FROG HUSBANDRY

Once equipped with a basic understanding of what poison dart frogs *are* (Chapter 1 and Chapter 3), where they *live* (Chapter 4), and what they *do* (Chapter 2) you can begin learning about their captive care.

Animal husbandry is an evolving pursuit. Keepers shift their strategies frequently as they incorporate new information and ideas into their husbandry paradigms.

There are few "right" or "wrong" answers, and what works in one situation may not work in another. Accordingly, you may find that different authorities present different, and sometimes conflicting, information regarding the care of these frogs.

In all cases, you must strive to learn as much as you can about your pet and its natural habitat, so that you may provide it with the best quality of life possible.

Chapter 5: Poison Dart Frogs as Pets

Poison dart frogs can make rewarding pets, but you learn all you can about them before adding one to your home. This includes not only understanding the nature of the care they require but also the costs associated with this care.

Assuming that you feel confident in your ability to care for a poison dart frog and endure the associated financial burdens, you can begin seeking your individual pet.

Understanding the Commitment

Keeping a poison dart frog as a pet requires a substantial commitment. You will be responsible for your pet's well-being for the rest of its life. When provided with proper care, most poison dart frogs will live for at least 4 to 6 years and many will live for twice or thrice as long. You must be prepared to care for your new pet for this entire time.

Can you be sure that you will still want to care for your pet several years in the future? Do you know what your living situation will be? What changes will have occurred in your family? How will your working life have changed over this time?

You must consider all of these possibilities before acquiring a new pet. Failing to do so often leads to apathy, neglect and even resentment, which is not good for you or your pet poison dart frog.

Neglecting your pet is wrong, and in some locations, a criminal offense. You must continue to provide quality care for your poison dart frog, even once the novelty has worn off, and it is no longer fun to clean the cage and provide him with insects each week.

Once you purchase a poison dart frog, its well-being becomes your responsibility until it passes away at the end of a long life, or you have found someone who will agree to adopt the animal for you. Unfortunately, this is rarely an easy task. You may begin with thoughts of selling your pet to help recoup a small part of your investment, but these efforts will largely fall flat.

While professional breeders may profit from the sale of poison dart frog, amateurs are at a decided disadvantage. Only a tiny sliver of the general population is interested in amphibian pets, and only a small subset of these are interested in keeping poison dart frogs.

Of those who are interested in acquiring a poison dart frog, most would rather start fresh, by *purchasing* a captive-bred individual from an established breeder, rather than adopting your questionable animal *for free.*

After having difficulty finding a willing party to purchase or adopt your animal, many owners try to donate their pet to a local zoo. Unfortunately, this rarely works either.

Zoos are not interested in your poison dart frog, no matter how pretty he is. He is a pet with little to no reliable provenance and questionable health status. This is simply not the type of animal zoos are eager to add to their multi-million-dollar collections.

Zoos obtain most of their animals from other zoos and museums; failing that, they obtain their animals directly from their land of origin. As a rule, they do not accept donated pets.

No matter how difficult it becomes to find a new home for your unwanted poison dart frog, you must never release non-native reptiles into the wild.

The Costs of Captivity

Amphibians are often marketed as low-cost pets. While true in a relative sense (the costs associated with dog, cat, horse or tropical fish husbandry are often much higher than they are for poison dart frogs), potential keepers must still prepare for the financial implications of amphibian ownership.

At the outset, you must budget for the acquisition of your pet, as well as the costs of purchasing or constructing a habitat. Unfortunately, while many keepers plan for these costs, they typically fail to consider the on-going costs, which will quickly eclipse the initial startup costs.

Startup Costs
One surprising fact most new keepers learn is the enclosure and equipment will often cost as much as (or more than) the animal does.

Prices fluctuate from one market to the next, but in general, the least you will spend on a healthy poison dart frog is about $50 (£35); you'll also need to spend at least $50 (£36) on his initial habitat and care equipment. Replacement equipment and food will represent additional (and ongoing) expenses.

Ongoing Costs
The ongoing costs of poison dart frog ownership primarily fall into one of two categories: food and maintenance. However, it is also important to plan for any veterinary care your pet may require.

Food costs are usually the most significant of the three, but they are relatively consistent and somewhat predictable. Additionally, many poison dart frog keepers will elect to raise their own feeder insects, which will reduce the costs associated with feeding your pet.

Some maintenance costs are easy to calculate, but things like equipment malfunctions are impossible to predict with any certainty. Veterinary expenses are hard to predict and vary wildly from one year to the next.

Food Costs

Food is the single greatest ongoing cost you will experience while caring for your poison dart frog. To obtain a reasonable estimate of your yearly food costs, you must consider the number of meals you will feed your pet per year and the cost of each meal.

The amount of food your poison dart frog will consume will vary based on numerous factors, including his size, the average temperatures in his habitat and his health.

Note that poison dart frogs typically feed on a large number of very small prey items. Because of the way feeder insects are usually priced (per individual, rather than per unit weight), it is actually more expensive to feed poison dart frogs than many other reptile and amphibian pets.

For example, a single poison dart frog may eat more than 100 individual insects in a week. It is very difficult to arrive at a yearly estimate for your food costs (especially given the wide variety of insects different hobbyists choose to feed their pet), but you'd be wise to budget at least $10 (£8) per week. You'll likely determine that your yearly costs are lower than this, but it is better to be safe than sorry.

Maintenance Costs

It is important to plan for both routine and unexpected maintenance costs. Commonly used items, such as paper towels, disinfectant and topsoil are rather easy to calculate. However, it is not easy to know how many burned out light bulbs, cracked misting units or faulty thermostats you will have to replace in a given year.

Those who keep their poison dart frog in simple enclosures will find that about $50 (£40) covers their yearly maintenance costs. By contrast, those who maintain elaborate habitats may spend $200 (£160) or more each year.

Always try to purchase frequently used supplies, such as light bulbs, paper towels and disinfectants in bulk to maximize your savings. It is often beneficial to consult with local amphibian-keeping clubs, who often pool their resources to attain greater buying power.

Veterinary Costs
There aren't a lot of services that veterinarians can provide to sick or injured poison dart frogs, but you should always seek assistance any time your pet's health declines.

While you should always seek veterinary advice at the first sign of illness, it is probably not wise to haul your healthy poison dart frog to the vet's office for no reason – they don't require "checkups" or annual vaccinations as some other pets may. Accordingly, you shouldn't incur any veterinary expenses unless your pet falls ill.

However, veterinary care can become very expensive, very quickly. In addition to a basic exam or phone consultation, your poison dart frog may need cultures, x-rays or other diagnostic tests performed. In light of this, wise keepers budget at least $200 to $300 (£160 to £245) each year to cover any emergency veterinary costs.

Myths and Misunderstandings
Unfortunately, there are many myths and misunderstandings about poison dart frogs. Some myths represent outdated

thinking or techniques, while other myths and misunderstandings reflect the desires of keepers, rather than the reality of the situation.

Myth: *Poison dart frogs are amphibians, so they are not capable of suffering or feeling pain.*

Fact: While it is important to avoid anthropomorphizing or projecting human emotions and motivations to non-human entities, amphibians – including poison dart frogs – feel pain. There is no doubt that they can experience pain and seek to avoid it. While it is impossible to know exactly what a poison dart frog thinks, there is no reason to believe that they do not suffer similarly to other animals, when injured, ill or depressed.

Myth: *Poison dart frogs lose their toxicity in captivity, so it is perfectly fine to hold them as much as you like.*

Fact: Despite losing their ability to produce poisons after being in captivity for a short time, poison dart frogs do not like to be handled or held. In general, they should be regarded as "hands off" pets.

Myth: *Poison dart frogs are good pets for young children.*

Fact: While poison dart frogs make wonderful pets for adults, teenagers and families, they require more care than a young child can provide. The age at which a child is capable of caring for a pet will vary, but children should be at least 12 years of age or so before they are allowed to care for their own dart frogs. Parents must exercise prudent judgment and make a sound assessment of their child's capabilities and maturity. Children will certainly enjoy pet amphibians, but they must be cared for by someone with adequate maturity. Additionally, it is important to consider the potential for young children contracting salmonella and other pathogens from the family pet.

Myth: *If you get tired of a poison dart frog, it is easy to find a new home for it. The zoo will surely want your pet; after all, you are giving it to them free of charge! If that doesn't work, you can always just release it into the wild.*

Fact: Acquiring a pet poison dart frog is a very big commitment. If you ever decide that your pet no longer fits your family or lifestyle, you may have a tough time finding a suitable home for it. You can attempt to sell the animal, but this is illegal in some places, and often requires a permit or license to do legally.

Zoos and pet stores will be reticent to accept your pet – even at no charge – because they cannot be sure that your pet does not have an illness that could spread through their collections. A zoo may have to spend hundreds or thousands of dollars for the care, housing and veterinary care to accept your pet poison dart frog, and such things are not taken lightly.

Some people consider releasing their poison dart frog into the wild if no other accommodations can be made, but such acts are destructive, often illegal and usually a death sentence for the animal.

Acquiring Your Poison Dart Frog

Modern amphibian enthusiasts can acquire poison dart frogs from a variety of sources, each with a different set of pros and cons.

Pet stores are one of the first places many people see poison dart frogs, and they become the de facto source of pets for many beginning keepers. While they do offer some unique benefits to prospective keepers, pet stores are not always the best place to purchase a pet amphibian; so, consider all of the available options, including breeders and swap meets, before making a purchase.

Pet Stores

Pet stores offer a number of benefits to keepers shopping for poison dart frogs, including convenience: They usually stock all of the equipment your new frog needs, including cages, heating devices and food items.

Additionally, they offer you the chance to inspect the poison dart frog up close before purchase. In some cases, you may be able to choose from more than one specimen. Many pet stores provide health guarantees for a short period, which provide some recourse if your new pet turns out to be ill.

However, pet stores are not always the ideal place to purchase your new pet. Pet stores are retail establishments, and as such, you will usually pay more for your new pet than you would from a breeder.

Additionally, pet stores rarely know the pedigree of the animals they sell, and they will rarely know the poison dart frog's date of hatching or other pertinent information.

Other drawbacks associated with pet stores primarily relate to the staff's inexperience. While some pet stores concentrate on amphibians and may educate their staff about proper poison dart frog care, many others provide incorrect advice to their customers.

It is also worth considering the increased exposure to pathogens that pet store animals endure, given the constant flow of animals through such facilities.

Reptile Expos
Reptile expos offer another option for purchasing poison dart frogs. Reptile expos often feature resellers, breeders and retailers in the same room, all selling various types of poison dart frogs and other reptiles.

Often, the prices at such events are quite reasonable and you are often able to select from many different poison dart frogs. However, if you have a problem, it may be difficult to find the seller after the event is over.

Breeders
Because they usually offer unparalleled information and support to their customers, breeders are generally the best place for most novices to shop for poison dart frogs. Additionally, breeders often know the species well and are better able to help you learn the husbandry techniques necessary for success.

The primary disadvantage of buying from a breeder is that you must often make such purchases from a distance, either by phone or via the internet. Nevertheless, most established breeders are happy to provide you with photographs of the animal you will be purchasing, as well as his or her parents.

Selecting Your Poison Dart Frog
Not all poison dart frogs are created equally, so it is important to select a healthy individual that will give you the best chance of success.

Practically speaking, the most important criterion to consider is the health of the animal. However, the age of the poison dart frog is also important to consider.

Health Checklist

Always check your poison dart frog thoroughly for signs of injury or illness before purchasing it. If you are purchasing the animal from someone in a different part of the country, you must inspect it immediately upon delivery. Notify the seller promptly if the animal exhibits any health problems.

Avoid the temptation to acquire or accept a sick or injured animal in hopes of nursing him back to health. Not only are you likely to incur substantial veterinary costs while treating your new pet, you will likely fail in your attempts to restore the poison dart frog to full health. Sick animals rarely recover in the hands of novices.

Additionally, by purchasing injured or diseased animals, you incentivize poor husbandry on the part of the retailer. If retailers lose money on sick or injured animals, they will take steps to avoid this eventuality, by acquiring healthier stock in the first place and providing better care for their charges.

As much as is possible, try to observe the following features:

- **Observe the animal's skin**. It should be free of lacerations and other damage. Pay special attention to those areas that frequently sustain damage, such as the front of the face. A small cut or abrasion may be relatively easy to treat, but significant abrasions and cuts are likely to become infected and require significant treatment.

- **Examine the animal's eyes and nostrils**. The eyes should not be sunken, and they should be free of discharge. The nostrils should be clear and dry – frogs who blow bubbles are likely to be suffering from a respiratory infection.

- Observe the animal's demeanor. Healthy poison dart frogs are aware of their environment and react to stimuli. When active, the animal should calmly explore his environment. Avoid lethargic animals, which do not appear alert.

The Age

Newly metamorphosized poison dart frogs are very fragile until they reach about three or four months of age. Before this, they are unlikely to thrive in the hands of beginning keepers.

Accordingly, most beginners should purchase four- or five-month-old juveniles, who have already become well established. In fact, if you can find and afford adults, it is often wiser still to purchase them.

Animals of this age tolerate the changes associated with a new home better than very young specimens do. They are also easier to feed. Further, given their larger size, they will better tolerate temperature and humidity extremes than smaller animals will.

Note that if you are planning to breed your poison dart frogs, you'll likely need to acquire a small group of animals. This is necessary because it is not possible to determine the sex of young frogs.

Accordingly, you'll want to purchase a group. This way, you'll be all but guaranteed to end up with members of each sex.

Quarantine

Because new animals may have illnesses or parasites that could infect the rest of your collection, it is wise to quarantine all new acquisitions. This means that you should keep any new animal as separated from the rest of your pets as possible.

Only once you have ensured that the new animal is healthy should you introduce it to the rest of your collection.

It is wise to obtain fecal samples from your poison dart frog during the quarantine period. You can take these samples to your veterinarian, who can check them for signs of internal parasites. Always treat any existing parasite infestations before removing the animal from quarantine.

Always tend to quarantined animals last, as this reduces the chances of transmitting pathogens to your healthy animals. Do not wash quarantined cage furniture with those belonging to your healthy animals. Whenever possible, use completely separate tools for quarantined animals and those that have been in your collection for some time.

Always be sure to wash your hands thoroughly after handling quarantined animals, their cages or their tools. Particularly careful keepers wear a smock or alternative clothing when handling quarantined animals.

Quarantine new acquisitions for a minimum of 30 days; 60 or 90 days is even better. Many zoos and professional breeders maintain 180- or 360-day-long quarantine periods.

Chapter 6: Providing the Captive Habitat

Providing your poison dart frog with appropriate housing is an essential aspect of captive care. In essence, the habitat you provide to your pet becomes his "world."

In "the old days," those inclined to keep frogs and other amphibians had few choices with regard to caging. The two primary options were to build a custom cage from scratch or construct a lid to use with a fish aquarium.

By contrast, modern hobbyists have a variety of options from which to choose. In addition to building custom cages or adapting aquaria, dozens of different cage styles are available – each with different pros and cons.

Dimensions

Throughout their lives, poison dart frog need a cage large enough to permit normal activity. In the case of most poison dart frogs, this usually means 1- to 4-square-feet of space. Young poison dart frogs and especially small species, however, may be able to live comfortably in less space than this.

But understand that these figures represent the *minimum* amount of space your pets require. It is almost always wise to offer the largest cage that you reasonably can.

Many keepers suggest that large cages are intimidating to frogs and other amphibians, but the truth is subtler. Contrary to the popular notion, large cages – in and of themselves – do not cause poison dart frogs to experience stress.

Poison dart frogs live in habitats that exceed even the largest cages by several orders of magnitude. What they do not do, however, is spend much time exposed, in wide-open habitats. Accordingly, you'll want to use a roomy enclosure, but be sure to fill it with plenty of natural-looking decorations.

Poison dart frogs do move around with relative abandon, thanks to their aposematic coloration and poisonous skin, but most prefer complex habitats, with plenty of visual barriers and places in which they can hide.

Aquariums

Aquariums are popular choices for poison dart frog cages, largely because of their ubiquity. Virtually any pet store that carries poison dart frogs will also stock aquariums.

Aquariums can make suitable poison dart frog cages, but they have a number of drawbacks. For starters, glass cages are hard to clean, and they are easy to break while you are carrying them around. Additionally, large aquariums are usually extremely heavy.

However, few habitats provide better viewing opportunities than aquaria, and because they're designed to hold water, they are a natural choice for poison dart frog enclosures featuring ponds, waterfalls, or other types of water features.

Note that you do not want to use a screened top with most poison dart frog habitats. Doing so will simply cause the habitat to dry out very quickly. Instead, you'll want to use a plastic lid designed for fish maintenance or cover the top with a flat piece of plastic. Just be sure to remove the top once every day or two to allow for proper air exchange.

Commercial Cages

Commercially produced cages have a number of benefits over other enclosures, but they do present a few drawbacks too.

For example, commercial cages usually feature doors on the front of the cage, allowing them to provide better access than top-opening cages do. Some commercial cages are made from transparent acrylic materials, while others are made from opaque plastic (aside from the front, which is usually made of acrylic).

Additionally, plastic cages are usually available in a greater variety of sizes than aquaria are, and often times, they are available with dimensions that are more suitable for terrestrial animals, like poison dart frogs. Aquaria are often quite tall with a relatively small footprint, whereas most commercial cages have a large footprint, but less height.

Commercially cages are available in two primary varieties: those that are molded from one piece of plastic and those that are assembled from several different sheets. Assembled cages are less expensive and easier to construct, but molded cages have few (if any) seams or cracks in which bacteria and other pathogens can hide.

Some cage manufacturers produce cages in multiple colors. Black is generally the best color to choose, when the option is available, as they do not show dirt very well. Additionally, poison dart frogs often look very sharp against black cage walls.

While poison dart frogs can likely see colors (to some degree), it is unlikely that cage color is a significant factor in their quality of life.

As with aquaria, you'll want to avoid commercial cages with large screened sections or other openings, as these will allow the moisture inside your frog's habitat to escape.

You needn't seal the habitat completely, and it is a good idea to allow periodic air exchange with the outside world, but you'll usually want to limit the amount of air that is allowed to escape from the habitat.

Plastic Storage Containers

Plastic storage containers, such as those used for shoes, sweaters or food, make suitable cages for poison dart frogs if they are customized to meet your frog's needs. However, you may need to alter the lid slightly to ensure your frogs do not escape.

It usually isn't necessary to drill ventilation holes in a plastic storage container. In fact, this will usually allow the humidity inside the container to drop to unacceptably low levels. In most cases, routine maintenance and feeding will provide more than enough air exchange for your frogs, and few storage boxes are truly air-tight anyway.

Homemade Cages

For keepers with access to tools and the desire and skill to use them, it is possible to construct homemade cages. However, this is not recommended for novice keepers, who do not yet have experience keeping poison dart frogs.

A number of materials are suitable for cage construction, and each has different pros and cons. Wood is commonly used but must be adequately sealed to avoid rotting, warping or absorbing offensive odors.

Plastic sheeting is a very good material, but few have the necessary skills, knowledge and tools necessary for cage construction. Additionally, some plastics may have extended off-gassing times.

Glass can be used, whether glued to itself or with used with a frame. Custom-built glass cages can be better than aquariums, as you can design them in dimensions that are appropriate for poison dart frogs. Additionally, they can be constructed in such a way that the door is on the front of the cage, rather than the top.

Chapter 7: Providing the Correct Lighting and Temperatures for the Habitat

Poison dart frogs require proper lighting and temperatures to thrive. And while these are both different environmental parameters, they often influence each other directly, as lights are often used to illuminate *and* heat a poison dart frog habitat.

Accordingly, we'll discuss lighting and heating your poison dart frog's habitat below.

Lighting

In most cases, poison dart frogs will thrive with nothing more than the ambient light entering the enclosure. The rainforest floor is a pretty dim environment, so they don't require (nor want) intense lighting.

However, your poison dart frogs will look much more attractive if you employ some type of lighting in the enclosure.

It is also important to consider the needs of the plants you install in the enclosure. While it is wise to select plants that have relatively modest light requirements for your poison dart frog habitat, most will thrive better if provided with high-quality lighting.

There are two basic ways to provide light for your dart frog's enclosure. You can use fluorescent lights or incandescent bulbs.

Fluorescent bulbs typically provide a better light-quality. They normally produce a more balanced light spectrum, which will make your frogs look their best.

However, fluorescent bulbs do not produce very much heat. So, while they are ideal for frog keepers who do not need to provide any additional heat to their frog's enclosure, they may require you to use additional heat sources in some cases.

An ordinary fluorescent bulb will suffice for your frog's habitat, but you can also select a premium model, designed to produce more balanced light. This will make the colors in the cage more appealing, and it may help your plants to stay healthier.

If you need to heat your dart frog's habitat, you may want to consider using incandescent bulbs instead of fluorescent ones. Incandescent bulbs produce a fair bit of heat, so be sure that you monitor the temperatures in side the habitat.

Heating Your Poison Dart Frog's Habitat

Providing the proper thermal environment is one of the most important aspects of poison dart frog husbandry. As ectothermic ("cold-blooded") animals, poison dart frogs rely on the surrounding temperatures to regulate the rate at which their metabolism operates.

Providing a proper thermal environment can mean the difference between a healthy, thriving pet and one who spends a great deal of time at the veterinarian's office, battling infections and illness.

While individuals may demonstrate slightly different preferences and different species have slightly different preferences, poison dart frogs prefer ambient temperatures in the mid-70s Fahrenheit (between 23 and 26 degrees Celsius). Temperatures for most species can be allowed to reach about 80 degrees Fahrenheit (26 degrees Celsius), but temperatures in the 85-degree Fahrenheit range (29 degrees Celsius) can be fatal.

In many cases, poison dart frog habitats can simply be left at room temperature. However, owners who live in cold regions or who maintain low temperatures in their homes may need to add heating devices to ensure a proper thermal environment for their pets.

Thermal Gradients

For the most part, poison dart frogs enjoy nearly ideal temperatures while living on the rainforest floor. They don't actively thermoregulate as much as many reptiles and some amphibians do. They don't appear to bask in the sunlight, for example. Such behaviors simply aren't necessary in most cases.

However, it is still wise to provide your frog with a range of temperatures inside the habitat so that he can access different temperatures if he likes.

The best way to do this is by clustering any heating devices used at one end of the habitat. The temperatures will slowly drop with increasing distance from the heating devices, which creates a *gradient* of temperatures.

Barriers, such as branches and vegetation, also help to create shaded patches, which provide additional thermal options.

This mimics the way temperatures vary from one small place to the next in your pet's natural habitat. By establishing a gradient in the enclosure, your captive poison dart frog will be able to access a range of different temperatures, which will allow him to manage his body temperature if necessary.

When setting up a temperature gradient, aim to make the warmest spot in the habitat about 80 degrees Fahrenheit (26 degrees Celsius). Ideally, the opposite end of the habitat should be about 70 degrees Fahrenheit (21 degrees Celsius).

Establishing a thermal gradient is easiest when using a roomy cage. In general, the larger the cage, the easier it is to establish a suitable thermal gradient.

Heating Equipment

There are a variety of different heating devices you can use to keep your poison dart frog habitat within the appropriate temperature range.

Be sure to consider your choice carefully and select the best type of heating device for you and your pet.

Heat Lamps

Heat lamps are commonly used to heat reptile and amphibian habitats, but they're usually overkill for poison dart frog maintenance. Additionally, because they require the use of a screened enclosure top in most cases, they're likely to dry out the habitat.

However, many plastic aquarium tops include fixtures for small incandescent bulbs. These types of enclosure lids can be very helpful for poison dart frog maintenance.

However, these types of lids can make it difficult to establish a thermal gradient, as the fixtures are usually situated near the middle of the habitat.

Accordingly, you'll need to monitor the habitat temperatures very carefully to ensure the habitat remains at the proper temperature range.

If you find that the temperatures are exceeding the desired range, you'll need to take steps to rectify the situation. The simplest way to adjust the temperature of your pet's cage is by changing the wattage of the bulb you are using.

For example, if a 15-watt light bulb is not raising the temperature of the basking spot high enough, you may try a 25-watt bulb. Alternatively, if a 40-watt light bulb is elevating the cage temperatures higher than are appropriate, switching to a 25-watt bulb may provide a better thermal environment.

Heat Pads

Heat pads are an attractive option for many new keepers, but they are not without drawbacks.

- Heat pads have a high risk of causing contact burns.

- If they malfunction, they can damage the cage as well as the surface on which they are placed.

- They are more likely to cause a fire than heat lamps or radiant heat panels are.

However, if installed properly (which includes allowing fresh air to flow over the exposed side of the heat pad) and used in conjunction with a thermostat, they can be reasonably safe. With heat pads, it behooves the keeper to purchase premium products, despite the small increase in price.

Heat Tape

Heat tape is somewhat akin to a "stripped down" heat pad. In fact, most heat pads are simply pieces of heat tape that have already been connected and sealed inside a plastic envelope.

Heat tape is primarily used to heat large numbers of cages simultaneously. It is generally inappropriate for novices and requires the keeper to make electrical connections. Additionally, a thermostat is always required when using heat tape.

Historically, heat tape was used to keep water pipes from freezing – not to heat amphibian cages. While some commercial heat tapes have been designed specifically for frogs and other small pets, many have not. Accordingly, it may be illegal, not to mention dangerous, to use heat tapes for purposes other than for which they are designed.

Heat Cables

Heat cables are similar to heat tape, in that they heat a long strip of the cage, but they are much more flexible and easy to use. Many heat cables are suitable to use inside the cage, while others are designed for use outside the habitat.

Always be sure to purchase heat cables that are designed to be used in frog habitats. Those sold at hardware stores are not appropriate for use in a cage.

Heat cables must be used in conjunction with a thermostat, or, at the very least, a rheostat.

Nocturnal Temperatures

Because poison dart frogs easily tolerate temperatures in the low-70s Fahrenheit (21 to 22 degrees Celsius) at night, most keepers can allow their pet's habitat to fall to ambient room temperature at night.

Because it is important to avoid using lights on your frog's habitat at night, those living in homes with lower nighttime temperatures will need to employ additional heat sources. Most such keepers accomplish this through the use of blue or red light bulbs, which provide heat, yet do not disturb the day-night cycle of your frogs.

Thermometers

It is important to monitor the cage temperatures very carefully to ensure your pet stays healthy. Just as a water test kit is an aquarist's best friend, quality thermometers are some of the most important husbandry tools for amphibian keepers.

Ambient and Surface Temperatures
Two different types of temperature are relevant for pet poison dart frogs: ambient temperatures and surface temperatures.

The ambient temperature in your animal's enclosure is the air temperature; the surface temperatures are the temperatures of the objects in the cage. Both are important to monitor, as they can differ widely.

Measure the cage's ambient temperatures with a digital thermometer. An indoor-outdoor model will feature a probe that allows you to measure the temperature at both ends of the thermal gradient at once. For example, you may position the thermometer at the cool side of the cage but attach the remote probe to a branch near the basking spot.

Because standard digital thermometers do not measure surface temperatures well, use a non-contact, infrared thermometer for such measurements. These devices will allow you to measure surface temperatures accurately from a short distance away.

Thermostats and Rheostats
Some heating devices, such as heat lamps, are designed to operate at full capacity for the entire time that they are turned on.

Such devices should not be used with thermostats – instead, care should be taken to calibrate the proper temperature by tweaking the bulb wattage.

Other devices, such as heat pads, heat tape and heat cables are designed to be used with a regulating device, such as a thermostat or rheostat, which maintains the proper temperature

Rheostats

Rheostats are similar to light-dimmer switches, and they allow you to reduce the output of a heating device. In this way, you can dial in the proper temperature for the habitat.

The drawback to rheostats is that they only regulate the amount of power going to the device – they do not monitor the cage temperature or adjust the power flow automatically. In practice, even with the same level of power entering the device, the amount of heat generated by most heat sources will vary over the course of the day.

If you set the rheostat so that it keeps the cage at the right temperature in the morning, it may become too hot by the middle of the day. Conversely, setting the proper temperature during the middle of the day may leave the morning temperatures too cool.

Care must be taken to ensure that the rheostat controller is not inadvertently bumped or jostled, causing the temperature to rise or fall outside of healthy parameters.

Thermostats

Thermostats are similar to rheostats, except that they also feature a temperature probe that monitors the temperature in the cage. This allows the thermostat to adjust the power going to the device as necessary to maintain a predetermined temperature.

There are two different types of thermostats:

- On-Off Thermostats

On-Off Thermostats work by cutting the power to the device when the probe's temperature reaches a given temperature.

For example, if the thermostat were set to 78 degrees Fahrenheit (25 degrees Celsius), the heating device would turn off whenever the temperature exceeds this threshold. When the temperature falls below 78, the thermostat restores power to the unit, and the heater begins functioning again.

This cycle will continue to repeat, thus maintaining the temperature within a relatively small range.

Be aware that on-off thermostats have a "lag" factor, meaning that they do not turn off when the temperature reaches a given temperature. They turn off when the temperature is a few degrees above that temperature, and then turn back on when the temperate is a little below the set point.

Because of this, it is important to avoid setting the temperature at the limits of your pet's acceptable range. Some premium models have an adjustable amount of threshold for this factor, which is helpful.

- Pulse Proportional Thermostats

Pulse proportional thermostats work by constantly sending pulses of electricity to the heater. By varying the rate of pulses, the amount of energy reaching the heating devices varies. A small computer inside the thermostat adjusts this rate to match the set-point temperature as measured by the probe. Accordingly, pulse proportional thermostats maintain much more consistent temperatures than on-off thermostats do.

Lights should not be used with thermostats, as the constant flickering may stress your pet. Conversely, heat pads, heat tape, radiant heat panels and ceramic heat emitters should always be used with either a rheostat or, preferably, a thermostat to avoid overheating your pet.

Thermostat Failure

If used for long enough, all thermostats eventually fail. The question is will yours fail today or twenty years from now.

While some thermostats fail in the "off" position, a thermostat that fails in the "on" position may overheat your frog. Unfortunately, tales of entire collections being lost to a faulty thermostat are too common.

Accordingly, it behooves the keeper to acquire high-quality thermostats. Some keepers use two thermostats, connected in a series arrangement.

By setting the second thermostat (the "backup thermostat") a few degrees higher than the setting used on the "primary thermostat," you safeguard yourself against the failure of either unit. This will help protect your pets from any thermostat failures, which may otherwise prove fatal.

This bumblebee poison dart frog is hunting for prey.

In such a scenario, the backup thermostat allows the full power coming to it to travel through to the heating device, as the temperature never reaches its higher set-point temperature.

However, if the first unit fails in the "on" position, the second thermostat will keep the temperatures from rising too high. The temperature will rise a few degrees in accordance with the higher set-point temperature, but it will not get hot enough to harm your pets.

If the backup thermostat fails in the "on" position, the first thermostat retains control. If either fails in the "off" position, the temperature will fall until you rectify the situation, but a brief exposure to relatively cool temperatures is unlikely to be fatal.

Chapter 8: Substrates

Substrates are used to give your poison dart frog a comfortable surface on which to crawl. Some will also absorb any liquids released by your frog. Substrates also serve as the bedding for any plants in the enclosure, and they can help create a realistic-looking habitat too.

There are a variety of acceptable choices, all of which have benefits and drawbacks. The only common substrate that is never acceptable is cedar shavings, which emits fumes that are toxic to reptiles.

Gravel

Gravel is used in two different ways by poison dart keepers. Some use it as their frog's sole substrate. Gravel won't absorb any liquids, and it can be difficult to keep clean, but it is the substrate of choice for some keepers.

Other keepers use gravel underneath soil or mulch, to provide a drainage layer for excess water added to the habitat. This way, the wood or soil above the gravel won't become waterlogged, which can lead to the proliferation of bacteria and accelerate the rate at which the substrate rots.

In either case, most keepers use very small gravel ("pea gravel"), but others worry that their frogs may inadvertently ingest these small pieces. Such keepers opt for larger pieces of gravel ("river rock"), which are far to large for your frog to swallow.

No matter how you use the gravel, you'll want to add a layer that is several inches thick, to provide enough room for water to collect without making your frogs or the substrate sit in standing water. Then, you'll simply pile substrate on top of the gravel, if you wish.

Note that by sloping the gravel, you can create depressions, hills, cliffs, and water basins. Just be creative and experiment until you arrive at a layout you like.

Soil

Organic potting soil or soil collected from a forested area can also be used in your poison dart frog enclosure. In fact, various soils are likely the most popular substrate choice among poison dart frog keepers.

Soil is easy to acquire, affordable (or free) and retains moisture well. It also allows you to install plants directly into the substrate.

Just be sure to collect the soil from an area that hasn't been exposed to pesticides or other chemicals, or, if you are purchasing the soil, opt for a variety that does not include perlite, fertilizers or other additives.

You can also make your own soil blend, by combining varying amounts of sand, peat moss and leaf litter. Just experiment with different proportions until you create a moisture-retaining mixture.

Moss

Various mosses, including sphagnum moss and Spanish moss, are used as a substrate by some poison dart frog keepers.

Mosses typically retain water very well, and therefore help to keep the humidity level in your frog's habitat high. However, they can be difficult to spot clean, and some types are rather expensive.

Moss also works well in decorative contexts, so you may want to use a gravel or soil substrate in your frog's habitat, and then simply add a bit of moss for aesthetic appeal.

Orchid Bark

The bark of fir trees is often used for orchid propagation, and so it is often called "orchid bark." Orchid bark is very attractive, although it is somewhat expensive.

Because orchid bark is often reddish in color, it is very easy to spot clean. However, monthly replacement can be expensive for those living in the eastern United States and Europe.

Orchid bark can be purchased from home improvement stores and floral supply channels, but you can also purchase versions specifically designed for reptile and amphibian habitats. There is no real difference in the mulch sold by various outlets, so you can simply look for the source with the most affordable pricing.

Cypress Mulch

Cypress mulch is a popular substrate choice for many tropical species, and it helps to provide a high humidity level, which is often beneficial for poison dart frogs.

Cypress mulch lasts for a very long time (even in damp conditions) without breaking down. Few plants will thrive when planted directly in cypress mulch. However, if you leave the plants in their pots, you can bury the pots in the cypress mulch to camouflage the pot.

One significant drawback to cypress mulch is that some brands (or individual bags among otherwise good brands) are comprised of narrow cypress bark sticks, rather than mulch composed of thicker pieces.

These sharp sticks can injure the keeper and the kept. It usually only takes one cypress mulch splinter jammed under a keeper's fingernail to cause them to switch substrates.

Paper Products

Paper-based substrates (including newspaper, newsprint and paper towels, as well as commercial paper products designed for vivaria maintenance) are very popular among reptile and, to a lesser extent, amphibian keepers, but they are not ideal for long-term use with poison dart frogs.

However, they can make a good substrate for temporary use or for quarantine cages in some cases. Use several layers of damp paper products to ensure sufficient cushioning and that your frog will not dehydrate.

Paper substrates are very easy to maintain, but they do not last very long and must be completely replaced when they are soiled. They must be changed regularly -- at least once per week, and often every day.

Chapter 9: Plants and Enclosure Furniture

You don't want to keep your poison dart frog in a barren enclosure. Bare enclosures are not only unattractive, they will fail to provide your frog with the type of microhabitats and visual barriers he needs to thrive. Additionally, like most other small animals, poison dart frogs need places in which they can hide – particularly at night. This is important for keeping their stress level low.

Accordingly, you'll want to include plenty of plants and several different types of furniture and decorations inside your poison dart frog's tank.

We'll talk about some of the best ways to use plants and furniture below.

Plants

Most poison dart frogs will fare better if you incorporate plants in their enclosure. Not only do plants provide your frogs with visual barriers and places to hide, they'll also help to keep the humidity level high and promote good air quality inside the habitat.

You can use artificial plants if you like, but while they will provide hiding places and make the habitat look nice to observers, they won't provide the other benefits live plants do.

You can plant cage plants directly in soil substrates or you can leave them in their containers. Most keepers prefer to install the plants directly in the cage substrate, and this is certainly acceptable. However, it does make substrate changes and cage maintenance slightly more difficult so be sure to think about all aspects of you dart frog's care before making a decision.

You must use care to select a species that will thrive in your dart frog's enclosure. For example, species that require direct sunlight will perish in the relatively dim light in your frog's habitat.

Instead, you must choose plants that will thrive in shaded conditions. Similarly, because you will be misting the cage regularly, and trying to keep the internal environment as humid as possible, few succulents or other plants adapted to arid habitats will live in a poison dart frog enclosure.

You must also consider the growth habit and characteristics of the plants you intend to use. For example, you'll want a combination of different plants, including ground covers, bushy plants and a few that grow vertically.

Most plants that lack dangerous spines should be safe for your poison dart frogs, however, it is always wise to consult with your veterinarian before selecting plants for the enclosure.

Some of the most common choices that are likely safe and well suited for your poison dart frog habitat include:

- *Pilea nummulariifolia*

- *Pelargonium* sp.

- *Camellia japonica*

- *Coleus* sp.

- *Hibiscus* sp.

- *Lavatera assurgentiflora*

- *Gynura aurantaca*

- *Tradescantia albiflora*

- *Dracaena deremensis*

- *Hoya exotica*

- *Calathea zebrina*

- *Astrophytum* sp.

- *Dracaena fragrans*

- *Codiaeum* sp.

- *Peperomia caperata*

- *Fuschia* sp.

- *Hoya exotica*

- *Impatiens* sp.

- *Saintpaulia ionantha*

- *Allyssum* sp.

- *Asperagus setaceus plumosis*

- *Aster* sp.

- *Helxine soleirolii*

- *Asplenium nidus*

- *Nephrolepsis exalta*

- *Callistemom* sp.

- *Bouganvillea* sp.

- *Tripogandra multiflora*

- *Aechmea* sp.

- *Bilbergia* sp.

- *Cryptanthus* sp.

- *Crassula argentea*

- *Fatsia japonica*

- *Lavandula officinalis*

- *Calendula officinalis*

- *Ruellia makoyana*

- *Graptopetalum paraguayen*

- *Carissa grandiflora*

- *Coleus* sp.

- *Areca* sp.

- *Chamaedorea elegans*

- *Tolmiea menziesii*

- *Pilea* sp.

- *Beaucarnea recurvata*

- *Maranta leuconeura*

- *Gynura* sp.

- *Chlorophytum comosum*

- *Platycerium bifurcatum*

- *Plectranthus australis*

- *Zinnia* sp.

No matter which species you select, be sure that you wash all plants before placing them in the enclosure to help remove any pesticide residues. It is also wise to discard the potting soil used for the plant. You'll obviously need to do so if you intend to install the plants directly in the substrate, but it is also a good idea to re-pot plants that you intend to keep inside containers too.

Considerations for Furniture and Decorations

Most poison dart frog keepers like to include hiding spaces, branches, logs, and other types of decorative items in their habitats.

While you can use a variety of different items to decorate your frog's habitat and provide him with visual barriers and hiding spaces, you must be sure to select items that satisfy a few key criteria:

- All furniture and decorations should be safe for your frog and feature no sharp edges or toxic chemicals.

- Items used as hides should accommodate the frog's body, but not much else. Most frogs prefer relatively small hiding spaces.

- Hides should have low profiles. Frogs often prefer to feel the top of the hide contacting the dorsal surface of their body.

- Hides either must be easy and economical to replace or constructed from materials that are easy to clean.

Common Decorative Items and Furniture

We'll talk about some of the best types of furniture and cage decorations to include in your habitat below.

Logs and Branches

Logs and branches make excellent decorations for poison dart frog enclosures. You can purchase climbing branches from pet and craft stores, or you can collect them yourself.

When collecting your own branches, try to collet those that are still attached to trees (always obtain permission first). Such branches will harbor fewer insects and other invertebrate pests than dead branches will.

Many different types of branches can be used in poison dart frog cages. Most non-aromatic hardwoods suffice.

Whenever collecting wood to be used as perches, bring a ruler so that you can visualize how large the branch will be, once it is back in the cage. Leave several inches of spare material at each end of the branch; this way, you can cut it to the correct length, once you arrive back home.

Always wash branches with plenty of hot water and a stiff, metal-bristled scrub brush to remove as much dirt, dust and fungus as possible before placing them in your frog's cage. Clean stubborn spots with a little bit of dish soap but be sure to rinse them thoroughly afterwards.

It is also advisable to sterilize branches before placing them in a cage. The easiest way to do so is by placing the branch in a 300-degree oven for about 15 minutes. Doing so should kill the vast majority of pests and pathogens lurking inside the wood.

Some keepers like to cover their branches with a water-sealing product. This is acceptable if a non-toxic product is used and the branches are allowed to air dry for several days before being placed in the habitat.

However, as branches are relatively easy to replace, it is not necessary to seal them if you plan to replace them.

Cork Bark
Real bark cut from the cork oak (*Quercus suber*), "cork bark" is a wonderful looking decorative item that can be implemented in a variety of ways.

Usually, cork bark is available in tube shape or in flat sheets. Cork bark may be slightly difficult to clean, as its surface contains numerous indentations and crevices. Use hot water, soap and a sturdy brush to clean the pieces.

Note that cork bark is often rather pricey, so you'll want to use it in the more visible areas of your frog's habitat.

Plant Saucers
The saucers designed to collect the water that overfills potted plants make excellent hiding locations. All you have to do is flip them upside down and cut a small opening in the side for a door.

Clay or plastic saucers can be used, but clay saucers are hard to cut. If you punch an entrance hole into a clay saucer, you must sand or grind down the edges to prevent hurting your pet.

As with plastic containers, you can attach decorative items, such as moss or bark, to the outside of plant saucers to improve their aesthetics.

Commercial "Half-Logs"
Many pet stores sell U-shaped pieces of wood that resemble half of a hollow log. While these are sometimes attractive looking items, they are not appropriate hide spots when used as intended.

The U-shaped construction means that the frog will not feel the top of the hide when he is laying inside. However, these hides can be functional if they are partially buried, thus reducing the height of the hide.

Commercially Produced Plastic Hides
Many different manufacturers market simple, plastic, hiding boxes. These are very functional if sized correctly, although some brands tend to be too tall. The simple design and plastic construction make them very easy to clean.

Plastic Storage Boxes

Just as a plastic storage box can be converted into an acceptable enclosure, small storage boxes can be converted into functional hiding places. Food containers, shoeboxes and butter tubs can serve as the base.

If the container has a low profile, it needs only have a door cut into the tub. Alternatively, you can discard the lid, flip the tub upside down and cut an entrance hole in the side.

Opaque containers are obviously preferable to transparent ones, but it is often easy to make clear containers opaque by covering them with paint or tape. You can also glue moss, mulch, bark or similar things to the outside to make the hides look better.

Cardboard Boxes

While they are not attractive, and you must discard and replace them anytime they become soiled, small cardboard boxes can also make suitable hide boxes – particularly on a temporary basis.

Just cut a hole in the side to provide a door. Just remember that cardboard will absorb moisture, so you'll need to replace cardboard hides frequently.

Paper Towel Tubes

Small sections of paper towel tubes make suitable hiding spots for poison dart frogs, although they should only be used on a temporary basis. They do not last very long, so they require frequent replacement. They often work best if flattened slightly.

Unusual Items

Some keepers like to express their individuality by using unique or unusual items as hiding spots. Some have used handmade ceramic items, while others have used skulls or turtle shells. If the four primary criteria previously discussed are met, there is no reason such items will not make suitable hiding spaces.

Chapter 10: Maintaining the Captive Habitat

Now that you have acquired your poison dart frog and set up his enclosure, you must develop a protocol for maintaining his habitat. While poison dart frog habitats require major maintenance every month or so, they only require minor daily maintenance.

In addition to designing a husbandry protocol, it is wise to employ a record-keeping system to track your poison dart frog's growth and health.

Cleaning and Maintenance Procedures

Once you have decided on the proper enclosure for your pet, you must keep your poison dart frog fed, hydrated and ensure that the habitat stays in proper working order to keep your captive healthy and comfortable.

Some tasks must be completed each day, while others are should be performed weekly, monthly or annually.

Daily
- Monitor the ambient and surface temperatures of the habitat.

- Spot clean the cage to remove any feces, urates or dead insects in the enclosure.

- Ensure that the lights, latches and other moving parts are in working order.

- Verify that your pet is acting normally and appears healthy. You do not need to handle him to do so.

Weekly
- Clean the inside surfaces of the enclosure.

- Clean any water dishes present with soap and water.

- Inspect your poison dart frog for any signs of injury, parasites or illness.

Monthly
- Break down the cage completely, remove and discard particulate substrates.

- Sterilize any water containers in use in a mild bleach solution.

- Weigh your poison dart frog.

- Photograph your pet (recommended, but not imperative).

- Prune any plants present in the enclosure as necessary.

Annually
- Replace the batteries in your thermometers and any other devices that use them.

Cleaning your poison dart frog's cage and furniture is relatively simple. Regardless of the way it became soiled, the basic process remains the same:

1. Rinse the object
2. Using a scrub brush or sponge and soapy water, remove any organic debris from the object.
3. Rinse the object thoroughly.
4. Disinfect the object.
5. Re-rinse the object.
6. Dry the object.

Chemicals & Tools
A variety of chemicals and tools are necessary for poison dart frog care. Save yourself some time by purchasing dedicated cleaning products and keeping them in the same place that you keep your tools.

Spray Bottles

Occasionally misting your pet's cage will ensure the enclosure doesn't become too dry. You can do this with a small, handheld misting bottle or a larger, pressurized unit (such as those used to spray herbicides). Automated units are available, but they are rarely cost-effective unless you are caring for a large colony of animals.

Small Brooms

Small brooms are great for sweeping up small messes and bits of substrate. It is usually helpful to select one that features angled bristles, as they'll allow you to better reach the nooks and crannies of your pet's cage and the surrounding area.

Ideally, the broom should come with its own dustpan to collect debris, but there are plenty of workarounds for those that don't come with their own.

Scrub Brushes or Sponges

It helps to have a few different types of scrub brushes and sponges on hand for scrubbing and cleaning different items. Use the least abrasive sponge or brush suitable for the task to prevent wearing out cage items prematurely. Do not use abrasive materials on glass or acrylic surfaces. Steel-bristled brushes work well for scrubbing coarse, wooden items, such as branches.

Spatulas and Putty Knives

Spatulas, putty knives and similar tools are often helpful for cleaning poison dart frog cages. Especially when it becomes necessary to remove things that have become stuck to the cage walls or furniture. Instead of trying to dissolve them with harsh chemicals, just scrape them away with a sturdy plastic putty knife.

Small Vacuums

Small, handheld vacuums are very helpful for sucking up the dust left behind from substrates. They are also helpful for cleaning the cracks and crevices around the cage doors. A shop vacuum, with suitable hoses and attachments, can also be helpful if you have enough room to store it.

Soap

Use a gentle, non-scented dish soap. Antibacterial soap is preferred, but not necessary. Most people use far more soap than is necessary -- a few drops mixed with a quantity of water is usually sufficient to help remove surface pollutants.

Bleach

Bleach (diluted to one-half cup per gallon of water) makes an excellent disinfectant. Be careful not to spill any on clothing, carpets or furniture, as it is likely to discolor the objects.

Always be sure to rinse objects thoroughly after using bleach and be sure that you cannot detect any residual odor. Bleach does not work as a disinfectant when in contact with organic substances; accordingly, items must be cleaned before you can disinfect them.

Veterinarian Approved Disinfectant

Many commercial products are available that are designed to be safe for their pets. Consult with your veterinarian about the best product for your situation, its method of use and its proper dilution.

Avoid Phenols

Always avoid cleaners that contain phenols, as they are extremely toxic to many small animals. In general, do not use household cleaning products to avoid exposing your pet to toxic chemicals.

Keeping Records

It is important to keep records regarding your pet's health, growth and feeding, as well as any other important details. In the past, keepers would do so on small index cards or in a notebook. In the modern world, technological solutions may be easier.

You can record as much information about your pet as you like, and the more information you record, the better. But minimally, you should record the following:

Pedigree and Origin Information

Be sure to record the source of your poison dart frog, the date on which you acquired him and any other data that is available. Breeders will often provide customers with information regarding the sire, dam, date of hatching and metamorphosis, weights and other records, but other sources will rarely offer comparable data.

Feeding Information

Record the date of each feeding, as well as the type of food item(s) offered. It is also helpful to record any preferences you may observe or any meals that are refused.

Weights and Length

Because you look at your pet frequently, it is difficult to appreciate how quickly he is (or isn't) growing. Accordingly, it is important to track his size diligently.

Weigh your pet with a high-quality digital scale. It is often easiest to use a dedicated "weighing container" with a known weight to measure your pet. Simply subtract the weight of the container to obtain the weight of your pet.

You can also measure your poison dart frog's length as well, but it is not always easy (or necessary) to do so.

Maintenance Information

Record all of the noteworthy events associated with your pet's care. While it is not necessary to note that you misted the cage every other day, it is appropriate to record the dates on which you changed the substrate or sterilized the cage.

Whenever you purchase new equipment, supplies or caging, note the date and source. This not only helps to remind you when you purchased the items, but it may help you track down a source for the items in the future, if necessary.

Breeding Information

If you intend to breed your poison dart frogs, you should record all details associated with pre-breeding conditioning, cycling, introductions and matings.

Record all pertinent information about any resulting egg clutches as well, including the number of viable offspring, as well as the number of eggs that fail to hatch into tadpoles.

Chapter 11: Feeding Poison Dart Frogs

Poison dart frogs are carnivorous animals (like all other adult frogs), who primarily feed on small invertebrates.

The best diet for captive dart frogs is one that mimics their wild diet, being primarily comprised of very small insects. It is very important to avoid feeding poison dart frogs prey items that are too large, as they have evolved to eat very large quantities of very small insects. Feeding them large insects is all but guaranteed to cause them intestinal impactions, which may be fatal.

You can feed your poison dart frog commercially produced insects or you can collect wild insects yourself. Both options have different benefits and drawbacks, which we'll discuss below.

Commercial Insects

There are a few different commercially produced insects that are suitable for feeding poison dart frogs. Some of the most popular options are discussed below.

Crickets

Crickets are likely the most popular prey item beginning poison dart frog keepers feed to their pets. Crickets are very affordable and they're usually available at most well-stocked pet stores. Additionally, it is easy to keep crickets alive for a week or so as you feed them off – simply provide them with a small dish of grains and an orange slice for moisture.

However, crickets do present some challenges. For starters, crickets are only small enough to serve as poison dart frog food for about one week. After this, they'll have grown too large for all but the biggest poison dart frogs. Additionally, hungry crickets are voracious animals, who may chew on your frog's body.

Accordingly, you'll need to identify a reliable source of young crickets. You can try to breed them yourself, but cricket rearing is more challenging than many beginning keepers would think. Additionally, crickets are notorious for creating offensive odors when kept in large numbers.

Additionally, if you ever introduce more crickets into the enclosure than your frogs can eat in a short period of time, you'll want to put some cricket food in the habitat too. This will help reduce the chances that they'll chew on your frogs.

Flightless Fruit Flies
Flightless fruit flies aren't as commonly fed by beginning dart frog keepers as crickets are, but most advanced poison dart frog keepers rely heavily on them.

Fruit flies don't grow too large for poison dart frogs, and they won't chew on your pets either. And because the types available to frog keepers lack the ability to fly, they're easy for dart frogs to catch.

The problem with feeding fruit flies is that you'll have to maintain a culture (or, more likely, several) of the flies to ensure that you have a steady supply of food.

Most fruit flies are sold in small tubes that contain an egg-laying substrate and food source for the flies. There may only be several dozen adult flies in the container at a given time, and you'll likely use most of the adults at each feeding.

However, a few days later, new fruit flies will hatch and start the cycle anew.

It isn't terribly difficult to maintain a fruit fly culture, but many beginners have trouble at the outset. However, with time and practice, most keepers eventually figure out how to maintain a healthy, productive fruit fly colony.

Wild-Caught Insects

There are a variety of insects and other invertebrates that you can collect and feed to your poison dart frogs. Some of the most appropriate choices are discussed below.

Isopods

Very small isopods ("roly polies") are acceptable food for poison dart frogs, and they're usually easy to collect. A five-minute stroll through a local forest will yield plenty if you simply look under a few decaying logs and flat rocks.

You can usually maintain isopods at home for a brief period of time if you provide them with a food source and suitable moisture. Note that isopods can also be helpful for your frog's habitat, as they'll help eat some of the decaying organic material in the enclosure.

Isopods don't represent a very big safety threat to your frogs. The most important thing to keep in mind is to avoid introducing large individuals into the habitat, as your frogs may try to eat them and end up choking.

Springtails

Springtails are small invertebrates (they are no longer considered insects), who have a spring-like appendage near their tail that helps them to jump.

Springtails are small enough to be suitable for poison dart frogs, and they are also relatively easy to collect – they're found in the same types of places that isopods are.

Springtails may also help to keep your dart frog's habitat clean, as they feed on decaying organic matter.

Termites

Termites are a very attractive food source for poison dart frogs, but it can be difficult to harvest them in significant numbers.

The best way to do so is by finding a small piece of rotting wood that is already infested with termites. You can then place the entire piece inside your frog's enclosure, so they can eat at their leisure.

Termites don't represent much of a threat to your poison dart frogs, and they are a nutritious food source.

Prey Size

It is vitally important that you provide your poison dart frog with feeder insects of the appropriate size. Fail to do so and your pets may become very sick – death is even possible in some cases.

This is important with adult poison dart frogs, but it is even more important when caring for juveniles. To avoid such problems, offer your frogs insects that are no longer than the distance between their eyes.

However, it is also important to watch your frogs closely when feeding them. Make sure that they appear to be acting normally and not under any duress after eating. If they become bloated or lethargic after eating, reduce the size of the insects provided immediately.

How to Offer Food

There are two basic ways to offer food to your poison dart frogs. You can simply dump an appropriate number of insects into the vivarium and allow your frog to chase them down and consume them.

However, you can also use a small feeding dish, and simply place the insects inside. This is more practical with termites and isopods than it is crickets of fruit flies, and it can be tricky to find a dish that is deep enough to keep the insects contained, yet shallow enough that your frog can easily capture them.

Nevertheless, this can be a helpful strategy for ensuring that your pets get enough to eat. It is especially helpful with young poison dart frogs, who sometimes struggle to capture prey.

Feeding Quantity and Frequency

Because they eat such small prey items, it can be surprising to see how many insects a mature poison dart frog can eat at one sitting. Many individuals will eat dozens of insects at a time.

Start by offering adult poison dart frogs about two dozen fruit flies or crickets. If they consume all of these feeders, add a few more to the habitat. Do this until the frog loses his interest in food.

You'll want to feed young poison dart frogs every day, but adults can thrive on four to five meals each week. And as long as your frogs are healthy and well-fed, the occasional multi-day fast won't harm them.

Vitamin and Mineral Supplements

Many keepers add commercially produced vitamin and mineral supplements to their frog's food on a regular basis. In theory, these supplements help to correct dietary deficiencies and ensure that captive frog's get a balanced diet. In practice, things are not this simple.

While some vitamins and minerals are unlikely to build up to toxic levels, others may very well cause problems if provided in excess. This means that you cannot simply apply supplements to every meal – you must decide upon a sensible supplementation schedule.

Additionally, it can be difficult to ascertain exactly how much of the various vitamins and minerals you will be providing to your pet, as most such products are sold as fine powders, designed to be sprinkled on feeder insects.

This is hardly a precise way to provide the proper dose to your frog, and the potential for grossly over- or under-estimating the amount of supplement delivered is very real.

Because the age, sex and health of your pet all influence the amount of vitamins and minerals he requires, and each individual product has a unique composition, it is wise to consult your veterinarian before deciding upon a supplementation schedule.

However, most keepers provide vitamin supplementation once each week, and calcium supplementation several times per week.

Chapter 12: The Water Needs of Poison Dart Frogs

Water is obviously necessary for all organisms, but it is especially important for amphibians, including poison dart frogs.

However, poison dart frogs – like most other frogs – do not drink water to remain hydrated. Instead, they absorb water from their environment through their skin and cloaca.

Accordingly, you needn't include a container of standing water in your frog's habitat (although many keepers choose to do so), as long as the humidity remains high enough.

We'll talk about some of the best ways to do this below.

Maintaining Proper Habitat Humidity

Poison dart frogs require fairly humid enclosures to thrive. Generally speaking, you'll want to shoot for a relative humidity between 80% and 95% at all times.

To maintain a high humidity level, you may need to employ any of several different techniques. We'll explain the most effective methods for maintaining proper humidity below.

Misting the Habitat

Simply spraying down the habitat with room-temperature water on a daily (or as-needed) basis will help to keep the habitat suitably humid.

Be sure that you only use bottled water, rain water, or water that has been treated with a dechlorinating product before using it in your frog's enclosure as chlorine can kill most amphibians.

You can simply use a hand-held spraying bottle if you only have one small habitat to tend, but if you have a large habitat or end up keeping several different dart frogs in their own enclosures, you may want to opt for a pressurized misting unit.

You can also install an automatic misting system. This is typically the easiest method for ensuring your frog habitat remains suitably humid, but many misting systems are rather expensive.

Adding Water to the Substrate
Simply adding water to a soil or mulch substrate will help maintain a high humidity level. However, you must use care to avoid making the substrate muddy or perpetually wet. You want the water inside the substrate to evaporate into the air, rather than remain in the substrate and create a soggy mess.

Accordingly, this can be one of the least labor-intensive, yet tricky methods of maintaining proper enclosure humidity. Note that you'll likely need to add water to the substrate regularly anyway, to ensure the plants remain healthy.

Reducing Ventilation
If you maintain a sealed habitat, any water you introduce to the enclosure will remain there. In fact, you would never have to add supplemental water again if you kept the habitat sealed.

But this is obviously not possible. Not only do your frogs need fresh air from time to time, you'll have to open the enclosure periodically to feed your pets and maintain the habitat.

But, you can help keep the internal humidity of the enclosure as high as possible by reducing the amount of ventilation provided.

Typically, this means covering large screened sections of the tank with plastic. Just be sure that you open the enclosure every other day or so, to provide your pets with fresh air.

Note that the larger the enclosure is, the less you'll have to open it to provide fresh air.

Adding a Large Water Feature

One of the simplest ways to increase the humidity in your frog's tank is by incorporating a large water reservoir in the enclosure.

By doing so, the water in the reservoir will evaporate over time, thereby releasing moisture into the air. You'll obviously have to add water to the reservoir over time, but this isn't terribly difficult to do.

In fact, the humidity provided by a large water reservoir is the primary reason some hobbyists incorporate ponds and waterfalls in their habitats.

Incorporating Live Plants

There are several reasons to include plants in your enclosure. We already discussed the way live plants can provide frogs with hiding places and visual barriers, and the fact that they improve the aesthetics of a dart frog habitat, but they also help to maintain a high humidity in the cage.

Plants do this by drawing water from the ground via their roots, and then releasing it into the air via a process called transpiration.

The more plants you include, the more water that they'll release into the air. Just realize that you'll have to add water to the substrate periodically to replace that which the plants have already absorbed.

Chapter 13: Interacting with Poison Dart Frogs

Assuming that they were born in captivity or have lived in captivity for a significant length of time, you can handle poison dart frogs. However, it is rarely necessary or advisable to use your hands when doing so.

Poison dart frogs are not "hands-on" pets, and you should generally treat them the same way you would treat a pet fish – watch and enjoy them but keep your hands off of them.

However, it will occasionally be necessary to handle your pet to move him or inspect his health. Accordingly, you'll need to learn the best ways to do so.

Handling a Poison Dart Frog

The very best way to handle your poison dart frog is to coax him into a small plastic cup.

Your hands are very rough and dry compared to your pet's skin, and unnecessary physical contact will cause him to become stressed. He may even become sick if handled roughly or too often.

Convincing him to hop into a cup, however, won't harm him, and it is usually easy to do. Simply place the lip of the cup on the ground in front of him and put your other hand behind him.

Usually, this is all that will be necessary – your pet will try to move away from your hand, and in doing so, he'll hop into the cup. If necessary, you can tap on the ground behind him. If this fails, lightly bump the rear portion of his body, and he'll likely move into the cup.

Transporting Your Pet

Although you should strive to avoid any unnecessary travel with your poison dart frog, circumstances often demand that you do (such as if your pet becomes ill).

Strive to make the journey as stress-free as possible for your pet. This means protecting him from physical harm, as well as blocking as much stressful stimuli as possible.

The best type of container to use when transporting your poison dart frog is a plastic storage box or cup.

Add a few damp paper towels to the container so your pet doesn't become dehydrated during the journey. These paper towels will also help absorb any fluids your frog releases during the journey.

Monitor your poison dart frog regularly but avoid constantly opening the container to take a peak. Checking up on your pet once every half-hour or so is more than sufficient.

Pay special attention to the enclosure temperatures while traveling. Try to keep the temperatures in the low-70s Fahrenheit (21 to 22 degrees Celsius) so that your pet will remain comfortable. Use the air-conditioning or heater in your vehicle as needed to keep the animal within this range.

Keep your poison dart frog's transportation container as stable as possible while traveling. Do not jostle your pet unnecessarily and always use a gentle touch when moving the container. Never leave the container unattended.

Because you cannot control the thermal environment, it is not wise to take your poison dart frog with you on public transportation.

Hygiene

Frogs can carry *Salmonella* spp., *Escherichia coli* and several other zoonotic pathogens and parasites. Accordingly, it is imperative to use good hygiene practices when performing habitat maintenance or feeding your pet. Always wash your hands with soap and warm water each time you touch your pet, his habitat or the tools you use to care for him. Antibacterial soaps are preferred, but standard hand soap will suffice.

In addition to keeping your hands clean, you must also take steps to ensure your environment does not become contaminated with pathogens. In general, this means keeping your poison dart frog and any of the tools and equipment you use to maintain his habitat separated from your belongings.

Establish a safe place to prepare your pet's food, store equipment and clean his habitat. Make sure the place is far from places human food is prepared. Never wash cages or tools in kitchens or bathrooms that are used by humans. Always clean and sterilize any items that become contaminated by the germs from your poison dart frog or his habitat.

Chapter 14: Common Health Concerns

Like many other amphibians, poison dart frogs are hardy animals, who often remain healthy despite their keeper's mistakes. In fact, most illnesses that befall pet poison dart frogs result from improper husbandry, and are, therefore, entirely avoidable.

Nevertheless, poison dart frogs often fail to exhibit any symptoms that they are sick until they have reached an advanced state of illness. This means that prompt action is necessary at the first hint of a problem. Doing so provides your pet with the greatest chance of recovery.

While proper husbandry is solely in the domain of the keeper, and some minor injuries or illnesses can be treated at home, veterinary care is necessary for many health problems.

It is important to note that there are not as many veterinary treatments available for frogs as there are for some other exotic pets. Most frogs (especially poison dart frogs) are small, which presents treatment challenges, and relatively few vets have accumulated a great deal of experience treating frogs either.

Accordingly, it is always better to prevent illnesses from occurring than it is to treat them once they've taken hold.

Finding a Suitable Vet

While any veterinarian – even one who specializes in dogs and cats – may be able to help you keep your pet helathy, it is wise to find a veterinarian who specializes in treating amphibians.

Such veterinarians are more likely to be familiar with your pet species and be familiar with the most current treatment standards for frogs and other amphibians.

Some of the best places to begin your search for a amphibian-oriented veterinarian include:

- Veterinary associations

- Local pet stores

- Local colleges and universities

It is always wise to develop a relationship with a qualified veterinarian before you need his or her services. This way, you will already know where to go in the event of an emergency, and your veterinarian will have developed some familiarity with your pet.

When to See the Vet

Most conscientious keepers will not hesitate to seek veterinary attention on behalf of their pet. However, veterinary care can be expensive for the keeper and stressful for the kept, so unnecessary visits are best avoided.

If you are in doubt, call or email your veterinarian and explain the problem. He or she can then advise you if the problem requires an office visit or not.

However, you must always seek prompt veterinary care if your pet exhibits any of the following signs or symptoms:

- Traumatic injuries, such as lacerations, burns, broken bones or puncture wounds

- Sores, ulcers, lumps or other deformations of the skin

- Intestinal disturbances that do not resolve within 48 hours

- Drastic changes in behavior

- Inability to deposit eggs

Remember that frogs are perfectly capable of feeling pain and suffering, so apply the golden rule: If you would appreciate medical care for an injury or illness, it is likely that your pet does as well.

Important Health Problems

The following are some of the most important health problems that afflict poison dart frogs. Be alert for any signs of the following maladies and take steps to remedy the problem.

Bacterial Infections

Given that poison dart frogs spend most of their time crawling around in damp soils and mosses, it isn't surprising that they can suffer from bacterial infections from time to time.

There are a number of different bacteria that can infect poison dart frogs, and the various bacteria can cause problems for different organ systems. Some bacteria can cause skin ailments for your frog, while others may cause intestinal issues.

Your dart frog may be able to fight off some of these bacteria on his own, but others will require antibiotics to treat. Some of the most common signs of bacterial infections include:

- Diarrhea

- Regurgitation / vomiting

- Skin discoloration (particularly of the ventral surfaces)

- Wounds that do not heal

- Lethargy

- Inappetence

If you note these or any other significant symptoms discuss the problem with your vet and heed his or her advice.

Fungal Infections

Like bacteria, fungi can also cause infections for frogs. In fact, one fungus in particular – colloquially called the frog chytrid fungus – is currently wiping out entire populations of frogs around the world.

Fungal infections can cause a wide variety of health problems for frogs. Some will experience systemic symptoms, ranging from lethargy to inappetence, while others will experience localized problems, which may afflict the skin, mouth, eyes or cloaca.

Fungal infections are sometimes very difficult to treat, and euthanasia may even be prudent in some cases. Accordingly, you'll want to do everything in your power to protect your frog from pathogenic fungi to avoid infections in the first place.

To do so, you'll want to use care when visiting other frog collections and be sure to wash your hands thoroughly before returning to your own pets.

Additionally, it is vital that you provide your frogs with the best care possible. This will help keep their immune system operating at peak efficiency and therefore give them the best chance to fight off infections before they take hold.

If you ever suspect that your frog is suffering from a fungal infection, contact your vet immediately.

Respiratory Infections
Respiratory infections aren't especially common health problems for frogs, but they can sicken poison dart frogs from time to time.

The most common symptoms of respiratory infections are discharges from the nose or mouth; however, lethargy, inappetence and behavioral changes may also accompany respiratory infections.

Myriad causes can lead to this type of illness, including communicable pathogens, as well as, ubiquitous, yet normally harmless, pathogens, which opportunistically infect stressed animals.

Your poison dart frog may be able to fight off these infections without veterinary assistance, but it is wise to solicit your vet's opinion at the first sign of illness. Some respiratory infections can prove fatal and require immediate attention.

Your vet will likely obtain samples, send off the samples for laboratory testing and then interpret the results. Antibiotics or other medications may be prescribed to help your poison dart frog recover, and your veterinarian will likely encourage you to keep the pet's stress level low and ensure his enclosure temperatures are ideal.

Internal Parasites
In the wild, most amphibians carry some internal parasites. While it may not be possible to keep a frog completely free of internal parasites, it is important to keep these levels in check.

Consider any wild-caught poison dart frog to be parasitized until proven otherwise. While most captive bred frogs should have relatively few internal parasites, they can suffer from such problems as well.

Most internal parasites that are of importance for poison dart frogs are transmitted via the fecal-oral route. This means that eggs (or similar life stages) of the parasites are released with the feces. If the frog inadvertently ingests these, the resulting parasites can develop inside his body and cause illness.

Such eggs are usually microscopic and easily lifted into the air, where they may stick to cage walls or land in the water dish. Later, when the frog grabs an insect, it ingests the eggs too.

Because cages that are continuously contaminated from feces are likely to lead to dangerous parasite loads, employ strict hygiene practices at all times.

Internal parasites may cause your pet to vomit, pass loose stools, fail to grow or refuse food entirely. Other parasites may produce no symptoms at all, which illustrates the importance of routine examinations.

Your veterinarian will usually examine your frog's feces if he suspects internal parasites. By looking at the type of eggs inside the pet's feces, your veterinarian can determine which medication will treat the problem.

Many parasites are easily treated with anti-parasitic medications, but often, these medications must be given several times to eradicate the pathogens completely.

Some parasites may be transmissible to people, so always take proper precautions, including regular hand washing and keeping reptiles and their cages away from kitchens and other areas where foods are prepared.

Examples of common internal parasites include roundworms, tapeworms and amoebas.

Injuries
Poison dart frogs can become injured in myriad ways. While they are likely to heal from most minor wounds without medical attention, serious wounds will necessitate veterinary assistance.

Your vet will likely clean the wound, make any repairs necessary and prescribe a course of antibiotics to help prevent infection. Be sure to keep the enclosure as clean as possible during the healing process.

Quarantine

Quarantine is the practice of isolating animals to prevent them from transferring diseases between themselves.

If you have no other pet amphibians (particularly other poison dart frogs), quarantine is unnecessary. However, if you already maintain other poison dart frogs you must provide all new acquisitions with a separate enclosure.

At a minimum, quarantine all new acquisitions for 30 days. However, it is wiser still to extend the quarantine period for 60 to 90 days, to give yourself a better chance of discovering any illness present before exposing your colony to new, potentially sick, animals.

Professional zoological institutions often quarantine animals for six months to a year. In fact, some zoos keep their animals in a state of perpetual quarantine.

Chapter 15: Breeding Poison Dart Frogs

Many dart frog keepers are intrigued at the idea of breeding their pets. While this is a fun, educational activity, you must prepare your frogs well for the activity to have any chance of success.

It is also important to be sure that you are ready to take care of any young that result from your efforts. Many keepers decide to try their hand at breeding, only to become stressed out at the notion of caring for a number of young tadpoles and, eventually, froglets.

You must also consider what you will do with all of these young. You may plan on selling the young to other frog enthusiasts, but this presents its own set of challenges.

Many municipalities require expensive permits to keep large numbers of amphibians – selling them requires other permits altogether. You may even have to learn how to ship poison dart frogs and obtain the necessary permits for that.

Additionally, you will have to spend money to advertise that you have frogs for sale. Ultimately, most beginners find that it is simply best to give away their poison dart frogs to other keepers.

Finally, you must consider the costs associated with housing a large number of tadpoles and froglets. Each will need its own food supply and enclosure.

Different Species Require Different Breeding Conditions

Note that while poison dart frogs are all closely related species, and they exhibit a number of similar traits, different species require different types of stimuli and environmental conditions to induce breeding activity.

Accordingly, you'll need to research the precise needs of the species you keep to have the best chance at producing young.

Nevertheless, we'll outline the basics of breeding poison dart frogs below.

Pre-Cycling Conditioning

Only poison dart frogs in perfect health should be considered for breeding trials. If a frog exhibits signs of stress, respiratory illness, mites, mouth rot or other illnesses, avoid breeding the animal until it is 100 percent healthy.

Prior to the breeding season, you'll need to feed adults slated for breeding trials heavily. Just avoid over-feeding them – overweight frogs make poor breeders.

Cycling

Like many other amphibians, poison dart frogs breed most reliably when cycled in a manner that mimics the seasonal changes in their native lands.

However, this may not always be necessary to trigger reproduction, and it is probably more important for those species and subspecies that live in areas with greater seasonal variation.

Species hailing from regions that don't experience much seasonal change are more likely to breed when kept under fairly consistent environmental conditions, while those hailing from areas with distinct seasons may require more significant environmental manipulation.

In most cases, poison dart frogs breed when the humidity and precipitation levels are at their highest. Often, these times of year follow relatively dry periods.

This means that it is often possible to induce breeding behaviors by allowing the humidity in your frog's habitat to drop slightly (do not allow the habitat to become excessively dry) for a few weeks. Then, begin misting the habitat heavily and maintain a very high habitat humidity.

With luck, you'll soon see your males perching and calling, and the females will soon begin depositing eggs.

Pairing

You can keep your frogs together all year long if you like, but some breeders have better luck by maintaining the sexes separately, and then introducing them for brief breeding periods.

It can sometimes be advantageous to keep several males in a breeding enclosure, as their competitive instincts may help trigger breeding behavior. However, it is usually wise to house females singly, as they may consume the eggs deposited by other females.

If you do decide to keep the sexes separate, you should probably introduce them to each other a few days before you begin misting them heavily.

Setting Up Egg-Deposition Sites

You'll have to set up a few places for your poison dart frogs to deposit and fertilize their eggs. There are a number of ways you can do so, but the most common method is as follows:

Place a small petri dish, glass ashtray or similar receptacle in an easily accessed portion of the habitat. Fill it with a small amount of dechlorinated water.

Poison dart frogs prefer to have a secluded place in which to carry out their breeding behaviors, so you'll want to then cover the water dish with some type of hide. Many keepers use half of a coconut shell. Just prop the end of the coconut shell up or cut a door into the side to provide the frogs with access to it.

Your frogs will also need a slightly larger water reservoir for the tadpoles, once they've hatched from their eggs. Note that many poison dart frog tadpoles are cannibalistic, so you'll likely want to remove them from the reservoir and rear them in individual cups.

Fertilization and Egg-Deposition

Poison dart frogs do not engage in amplexus like most other frogs do. Instead, the male will discharge sperm into a water source and the female will then deposit an egg mass into the water source.

The males of some species will return several times over the next few days to urinate on the eggs, thereby preventing them from desiccating. About one to two weeks later, the eggs will begin to hatch.

At this time, the male will usually carry the eggs from the egg deposition site to a larger body of water, however there is some variation in these behaviors – some species exhibit slightly different patterns.

Tadpole and Froglet Husbandry

Establish tadpole rearing containers for the young poison dart frogs several days before you expect them to hatch. The containers needn't be very large (a typical deli cup is usually ideal), and they should contain only dechlorinated water and perhaps a small plant cutting.

Most poison dart frog tadpoles can be fed a combination of fish flakes and Indian almond leaves.

As the tadpoles begin metamorphosis, you'll begin to see legs sprout. Once they have all four legs and start absorbing their tails, you can tilt the plastic deli cups slightly, which will allow the frogs to climb out when the time is right (just be sure that the cups are in a larger container to prevent the frogs from getting away).

The froglets should be set up in individual deli cup habitats or small plastic storage boxes. Feed them very small insects on a daily basis and be sure to maintain a high humidity in the enclosure, as young froglets can dehydrate very quickly.

A large blue poison dart frog surveys his surroundings.

By about two to three months of age, most young poison dart frogs are large enough to be sold or given away to friends.

Just be sure that if you decide to keep any for future breeding projects that you select only the hardiest young specimens possible.

Weak froglets rarely mature into strong breeders. It is likely than many such frogs fail to survive long enough to reach maturity in the wild.

Chapter 16: Further Reading

Never stop learning more about your new pet's natural history, biology and captive care. This is the only way to ensure that you are providing your new frogs with the highest quality of life possible.

It's always more fun to watch your poison dart frogs than to read about them, but by accumulating more knowledge, you'll be better able to provide him with a high quality of life.

Books

Bookstores and online book retailers offer a treasure trove of information that will advance your quest for knowledge. While books represent an additional cost involved in reptile and amphibian care, you can consider it an investment in your pet's well-being. Your local library may also carry some books about poison dart frogs, which you can borrow for no charge.

University libraries are a great place for finding old, obscure or academically oriented books about poison dart frogs. You may not be allowed to borrow these books if you are not a student, but you can view and read them at the library.

Herpetology: An Introductory Biology of Amphibians and Reptiles
By Laurie J. Vitt, Janalee P. Caldwell
Top of Form
Bottom of Form
Academic Press, 2013

Designer Reptiles and Amphibians
Richard D. Bartlett, Patricia Bartlett
Barron's Educational Series

Magazines

Because magazines are typically published monthly or bi-monthly, they occasionally offer more up-to-date information than books do. Magazine articles are obviously not as comprehensive as books typically are, but they still have considerable value.

Reptiles Magazine

www.reptilesmagazine.com/

Covering reptiles and amphibians commonly kept in captivity.

Practical Reptile Keeping

http://www.practicalreptilekeeping.co.uk/

Practical Reptile Keeping is a popular publication aimed at beginning and advanced hobbies. Topics include the care and maintenance of popular reptiles and amphibians as well as information on wild populations.

Websites

The internet has made it much easier to find information about amphibians than it has ever been.

However, you must use discretion when deciding which websites to trust. While knowledgeable breeders, keepers and academics operate some websites, many who maintain amphibian-oriented websites lack the same dedication to scientific rigor.

Anyone with a computer and internet connection can launch a website and say virtually anything they want about poison dart frogs. Accordingly, as with all other research, consider the source of the information before making any husbandry decisions.

The Reptile Report
www.thereptilereport.com/
The Reptile Report is a news-aggregating website that accumulates interesting stories and features about reptiles and amphibians from around the world.

Kingsnake.com
www.kingsnake.com
After starting as a small website for gray-banded kingsnake enthusiasts, Kingsnake.com has become one of the largest reptile- and amphibian-oriented portals in the hobby. The site features classified advertisements, a breeder directory, message forums and other resources.

The Vivarium and Aquarium News
www.vivariumnews.com/
The online version of the former print publication, The Vivarium and Aquarium News provides in-depth coverage of different reptiles and amphibians in a captive and wild context.

Journals
Journals are the primary place professional scientists turn when they need to learn about poison dart frogs. While they may not make light reading, hobbyists stand to learn a great deal from journals.

Herpetologica
www.hljournals.org/
Published by The Herpetologists' League, Herpetologica, and its companion publication, Herpetological Monographs cover all aspects of reptile and amphibian research.

Journal of Herpetology
www.ssarherps.org/
Produced by the Society for the Study of Reptiles and
Amphibians, the Journal of Herpetology is a peer-reviewed
publication covering a variety of reptile- and amphibian-
related topics.

Copeia
www.asihcopeiaonline.org/
Copeia is published by the American Society of Ichthyologists
and Herpetologists. A peer-reviewed journal, Copeia covers
all aspects of the biology of reptiles, amphibians and fish.

Nature
www.nature.com/
Although Nature covers all aspects of the natural world, many
issues contain information that poison dart frog enthusiasts
are sure to find interesting.

Supplies
You can obtain most of what you need to maintain poison dart
frogs through your local pet store, big-box retailer or
hardware store, but online retailers offer another option.

Just be sure that you consider the shipping costs for any
purchase, to ensure you aren't "saving" yourself a few dollars
on the product yet spending several more dollars to get the
product delivered.

Big Apple Pet Supply
http://www.bigappleherp.com
Big Apple Pet Supply carries most common husbandry
equipment, including heating devices, water dishes and
substrates.

LLLReptile

http://www.lllreptile.com

LLL Reptile carries a wide variety of husbandry tools, heating devices, lighting products and more.

Doctors Foster and Smith

http://www.drsfostersmith.com

Foster and Smith is a veterinarian-owned retailer that supplies husbandry-related items to pet keepers.

Support Organizations

Sometimes, the best way to learn about poison dart frogs is to reach out to other keepers and breeders. Check out these organizations, and search for others in your geographic area.

The National Reptile & Amphibian Advisory Council

http://www.nraac.org/

The National Reptile & Amphibian Advisory Council seeks to educate the hobbyists, legislators and the public about reptile and amphibian related issues.

American Veterinary Medical Association

www.avma.org

The AVMA is a good place for Americans to turn if you are having trouble finding a suitable reptile veterinarian.

The World Veterinary Association

http://www.worldvet.org/

The World Veterinary Association is a good resource for finding suitable reptile veterinarians worldwide.

References

Caldwell, J. P. (1996). The evolution of myrmecophagy and its correlates in poison frogs (Family Dendrobatidae). *Journal of Zoology*.

Catherine R. Darst, P. A.-G. (2004). Evolution of Dietary Specialization and Chemical Defense in Poison Frogs (Dendrobatidae): A Comparative Analysis. *The American Naturalist*.

Clough, K. S. (2001). The evolution of coloration and toxicity in the poison frog family (Dendrobatidae). *Proceedings of the Natural Academy of Sciences*.

Daly, J. W. (1982). Alkaloids of Neotropical Poison Frogs (Dendrobatidae). *Progress in the Chemistry of Natural Organic Products*.

Donnelly, M. A. (1991). Feeding Patterns of the Strawberry Poison Frog, Dendrobates pumilio (Anura: Dendrobatidae). *Copeia*.

John W.Daly, C. W. (1987). Further classification of skin alkaloids from neotropical poison frogs (dendrobatidae), with a general survey of toxic/noxious substances in the amphibia. *Toxicon*.

John W.DalyaSherrie I.Secunda, H. G. (1994). An uptake system for dietary alkaloids in poison frogs (Dendrobatidae). *Toxicon*.

MariaNeuwirth, J. W. (1979). Morphology of the granular secretory glands in skin of poison-dart frogs (Dendrobatidae). *Tissue and Cell*.

Miguel Vences, J. K.-H. (2000). Phylogeny and Classification of Poison Frogs (Amphibia: Dendrobatidae), Based on

Mitochondrial 16S and 12S Ribosomal RNA Gene Sequences. *Molecular Phylogenetics and Evolution.*

Monica Mensah-Dwumah, J. W. (1978). Pharmacological activity of alkaloids from poison-dart frogs (dendrobatidae). *Toxicon.*

Moreira, A. P. (1993). Effects of prey size and foraging mode on the ontogenetic change in feeding niche ofColostethus stepheni (Anura: Dendrobatidae). *Oecologica.*

Myers, C. W., & Daly, J. W. (1976). Preliminary evaluation of skin toxins and vocalizations in taxonomic and evolutionary studies of poison-dart frogs (Dendrobatidae). *Bulletin of the AMNH.*

Rand, J. W. (1994). Dietary source for skin alkaloids of poison frogs (Dendrobatidae). *Journal of Chemical Ecology.*

Roithmair, M. E. (1992). Territoriality and Male Mating Success in the Dart-poison Frog, Epipedobates femoralis (Dendrobatidae, Anura). *Ethology.*

Taran Grant, e. a. (2006). PHYLOGENETIC SYSTEMATICS OF DART-POISON FROGS AND THEIR RELATIVES (AMPHIBIA: ATHESPHATANURA: DENDROBATIDAE). *Bulletin of the American Museum of Natural History.*

Toft, C. A. (1995). Evolution of Diet Specialization in Poison-Dart Frogs (Dendrobatidae). *Herpetologica.*

W.Myers, J. W.-D. (1978). Classification of skin alkaloids from neotropical poison-dart frogs (dendrobatidae). *Toxicon.*

WEYGOLDT, P. (1987). Evolution of parental care in dart poison frogs (Amphibia: Anura: Dendrobatidae) . *Journal of Zoological Systematics.*